L AMB

Also by Frannie Lindsay

Where She Always Was, 2004

Lamb

FRANNIE LINDSAY

PERUGIA PRESS
FLORENCE, MASSACHUSETTS
2006

Perugia Press extends deeply felt thanks to the many individuals whose generosity made the publication of *Lamb* possible. For more information about Perugia Press, a nonprofit corporation publishing first and second books by women, and to make a tax-deductible donation, please contact us directly or visit our web site.

Grateful acknowledgment is made for permission to quote from "I Would Live in Your Love," by Sara Teasdale. Reprinted with permission of Scribner, an imprint of Simon & Schuster Adult Publishing Group from *The Collected Poems of Sara Teasdale* (New York: Macmillan, 1937).

Cover image is "Lamb," watercolor and ink, by Sarkis Antikajian, used with permission of the artist (www.sarkisantikajian.com).

Author photo by Meg Birnbaum.
Book Design by Jeff Potter/Potter Publishing Studio and Susan Kan.

Library of Congress Cataloging-in-Publication Data

Lindsay, Frannie.

Lamb / Frannie Lindsay.

p. cm.

ISBN-13: 978-0-9660459-9-4 (alk. paper)

I. Title.

PS3612.I533L36 2006

811'.6--dc22

2006007753

Perugia Press

P.O. Box 60364

Florence, MA 01062

info@perugiapress.com

http://www.perugiapress.com

For my sisters, all of them

ACKNOWLEDGMENTS

I am grateful to the following periodicals in which these poems first appeared:

The Atlantic Monthly: "Now"

Beloit Poetry Journal: "Receiving the Host"

Field: "Eighteen Lambs"

Harvard Divinity Bulletin: "Beatitude"; "Because I Asked"; "The Ewe Lamb"

Harvard Review: "Curse"; "Altar"

Hunger Mountain: "The Nativity of the Animals"; "Something He Did"

Passages North: "The Chores"; "Pants"; "Mother's Body, November"; "The Stops"

Poet Lore: "Mother Leaving, 1965"; "Saying Amen to My Father"

Prairie Schooner: "Clean"; "I found a boy"; "Thirty-Year Meditation on an Act of Violence"; "Crying"

Salamander: "Ordinary Mind"; "Henry"; "My father says"

Saranac Review: "Pas de Deux"

Spoon River Poetry Review: "Father in Darkness"; "My Duck"

Valparaiso Poetry Review: "Talking to My Father about God"; "Walking an Old Woman into the Sea"

The Yale Review: "Hatchling"; "God"

I am also indebted to Ellen Bass, Susan Nissbaum Becker, Paula Bohince, Terry Jane England, Jennifer Johnson, Ann Killough, Fred Marchant, Liz Moore, Sue Roberts, Aimée Sands, and Bruce Weigl for their dedicated and critical attention to this manuscript in its formative stages. Very special thanks to Jean Valentine and Chase Twichell, and to Susan Kan.

Contents

III.   THE STOPS

LAMB

THE EWE LAMB

— *2 Samuel 12: 3*

I raised my one ewe lamb
as a daughter, fed her
red clover, the last hearts
of my cabbage, offered
her inky lips my cup.
She rested her chin
on my neck at night, her hoofs
on my cloak, her breathing
the wind on the waves
of sleep's pure waters.
Sleep: an animal's word
for *bless:* hoof of her heart
to the hoof of my heart.
The dusk before her slaughter
we walked together, pauper
and kin, over the meadow.
I sang to her, then
I unstrung the rusted bell
from her collar.

I

Good, Good
Daughter

THIRTY-YEAR MEDITATION
ON AN ACT OF VIOLENCE

Sun through my white skirt,
trees with their backs turned,

boot prints I knew had been
on the stairs all this time;

air that believed me, weeknight air
I breathed a minute ago,

oh unsweet dark, if my eyes
never close again on their own

I will keep the broken-off
piece of my key, the child's tooth

under its pillow; do you
have the rest, the part

the lock knows
by feel, and can you

give it to someone
for me?

FATHER IN DARKNESS

Sometimes when we were the only ones left
awake, I could make my nipples stay soft
if I breathed without moving
my ribs when he lifted my p.j. top
and rubbed my back's edges,
right to left, palm bumping into
my steep, chilly shoulder blades,
making him stop
to cry and tell me he loved me,
then left to right again.

THE LOOKING

I said I would never again
eat her warm peach cobbler;
then I left the table
and went to my room
and instead of reading my book
for school, took off all my clothes
and stood sapling-tall
in the up-and-down mirror
and pinched the skin
at my waist and thighs,
facing sideways
then front, then turned
to examine the untidy
swerve of my rear;
did this over and over,
the looking; then pinched more
of *it,* of *it,*
and played with my hair
up close until the brittle ends
stared at long enough
could start a fire.

Mother Leaving, 1965

She would lay down her fork
in her mashed potatoes, swipe all the red
off her lips, and slip her chair out
from the brute-legged table. Then

she would brush the screen door's aching wing,
and dressed in the same pale shirtwaist
she'd worn every other spring night,
would take herself weeping
around the block for ten obedient minutes

and come promptly back as if she'd been sitting
right there among us, paying
just enough attention to pass the basket
of plump yellow rolls.

ORDINARY MIND

I don't know the word *jocund*
means *glad, joyful, cheerful,* or *lively,* and can't
think up a sentence including it.
Mrs. Champ scolds me and makes me
stand by the cloakroom door to think
about why I never follow directions.
I am aboard the crashing plane
of my fourth-grade classroom, counting
my cardigan buttons and gripping a rag
of breath. Through all the windows
at once, the playground has tilted
cheerfully sideways.

Shot

Ever since I was five, the man of my dreams
has been telling me *don't be afraid, I won't
hurt you.* I still think

polio shots are romantic.
I envied the girl ahead in the shot line,
balling the front of her red poodle skirt

in her fists, and hiding her face
in the pediatrician's angelic broadcloth.
The gymnasium smelled of isopropyl

and sacrament, and one of the mothers
brought in the newest Rosemary Clooney record
to calm us all down. I can't get the lyrics

out of my head. I have bitten my lip
for fifty years.

BLACKIE

for Rosie

The old guinea pig is not herself and so
you set her down on the counter,
and feed her a strawberry

over the sink in your glittery jeans. She was
a Christmas gift to the capable hands
a second grader has for wanting.

The glance of the Magi's Star in the vanity
mirror of the world in your room,
your mother brushing your hair

in the morning. Your heavy pink comb
in her quaking fur. Her eyes are still clear, but
tomorrow your father will help you carry

her cage to the basement. Tonight
you must hurry; you have a dance to get to.

CLEAN

She stood in the tub beside me again
a little slouched over her workaday belly

teaching me how a grown-up girl
must always clean herself:

she made a paw of her washcloth
and rubbed it back and forth inside,

she had me try it too in front of her;
then she helped me climb out

and dried me until I could stop
my shivering; she folded my peach-

colored towel over hers

DOLL

I twirled my Christmas doll Judith so hard
by her arm that the beige rubber finally thinned
and tore at the shoulder.

I hacked off her Dynel curls, gave her
a crew cut. I did not stash her
under my bed. Instead, I slit her pink

checkered smock and bonnet and left her
like that near the floor vent, the shells
of her eyelids shut.

The metal-rimmed holes
where the water went into her mouth
and came out of her bottom

rusted. I'm sorry for hapless objects,
a rain-pummeled mitten, a lamp set out
in the trash.

I spanked her; I stepped on her.
There is nothing to understand.

CURSE

I like your not liking me. The clink of your eyes
when they catch on my neck,
and the ravel. Perfect.

Look at you: spiffed and pasty, content
with bittersweet chocolate smattered with strings
of orange. Snap me a piece;

I will still have caught you
picking your teeth with the end of a Kleenex
you spit on and twist.

What can my girlie curse do to you?
Plenty. Nothing you'll notice.

SALVAGE

One day old, a kitten
the size of a sunfish

poisoned by milk
from its poisoned mother

and slick with placenta,

swims in its sleep
in the waves

of the blue towel
with stars on it.

Hatchling

I could not bury him, not
by the schoolyard's

sparking forsythia,

or offer him up
to the bored, clear sky,

so I held him as long as the sun
stayed warm on the palm

of a grocery bag, and watched him

shiver to nothing; and
was not sickened

by his crushed tongue and
cracked yellow beak

or his birthless legs' limp ferns

or the wrong way crook of his
his red-knuckled wings,

or the moist, contented lips
of his eyes

or his supple and broken neck
that I stroked

with the bill of my fingernail.

SUMMONING THE WHIPPOORWILLS

Just as the sun
went down,
he'd signal
his whippoorwills;
night by cooler
night, teach them
his whistle
so they could perfect
its shiver, then
dip, then
tritone slide
back up, and
by summer's end
call him first.

SOMETHING HE DID

One day when nobody else was home
my father polished off the last of the beer,

stripped down to just his cuffed dungarees
and stood on the porch and quit thinking

long enough
to shut out the bird noise, then struck

with his father's ten-pound ax
again and again what would have been

the pear tree's waist if it were a girl.

ELEVENTH SUMMER

I dove from his sunburned shoulders
and swam between his legs.

A swarm of minnows shattered. Gray pebbles
skinned my shadow's rudder.

The lake was calm and umber.
He said I was beautiful, after, up to my neck

in water, treading, smiling, doing it over
for him, for fun, daughter

and captor, the beautiful
day when death began.

THE CHORES

for Liz

My father sets the box of newborn kittens
into the pit of soil. I've done a good job
with his shovel.

He pats my bottom. I've tucked the right bullets
into the pouch of my overalls. He lets me
load the revolver, closes his hands around mine

from behind. The gravel and silo and sky
run together with mewing.
Eggs over easy sputter and clap from the kitchen.

I push the loose hair from my face,
aim down. The morning air is slow
with green flies. The straps of my first bra

pinch my shoulders. I am his
good, good daughter. *Now,* he says,
and I don't waste a shot.

SAYING AMEN TO MY FATHER

Finally one spring I was less afraid
to climb the crabapple tree,
its elbows knotted and able to take
the unfolding hand of my body, ready
to grip the next branch up

until, should I want to, I could
reach from the thick of all
that precarious white about to be fruit
into his study window; and then
using only

a stick of blossoms,
close the book in his lap, flick the afghan
over his rising and falling shoulders,
and blow out the lamp with a kiss
that touched nothing.

II

Beatitude

FRIEND

An old blonde dog takes care of me.
I found him starving in the snow.

His face is scarred, his hips protrude.
His joints are stiff. Doddering along,

he lists a bit, and more and more
he is incontinent.

Yet when I'm most alone, he brings me
his old polar bear, the sock

he likes to chew. His white chin fits
my darkest aches, and settles there.

Eighteen Lambs

Dedham Animal Sanctuary,
April 2004

She won't let me touch the lambs, the eighteen
she hauled here over the snapping gravel
in her pitch green truck,
at two in the morning,

not bleating, their cheek wool spiked
with spittle; their shut-mouthed smiles;
the scuffed nun shoes of their hooves.
The black one who lies on his side

in the hay and the shit. The two who butt
under the thinnest ewe's shorn rump,
and clamp their suede lips tight
on one distended tit, to fight

and feed. The jerking thumbs of their tails.
No lifting them up in thick towels, each
to its own nippled bottle. The fence
pierces the moss's pelt

and keeps me away from her lambs:
their dense, vacant faces, their tired breath
on the weave of the wire cut into
my hands. No lifting them.

God

for David

My friend is going to kill
his old appaloosa mare next week.
The horse won't eat, is down
to a few hundred pounds,
all sores and hips.

He and his wife have hired a boy
with a backhoe to cover her up
with the dirt's deep breaths. They know
how many grams of morphine
she's going to need.

They will let their daughter stay home,
she is old enough. And the mare,
who stands hour by hour in her stall
like a fire-damaged piano
knows all

about frost on the hay,
the achy barn door that reached
as far as it could every single day
with willingness, leading the same
enormous morning in.

I FOUND A BOY

who had no blanket   no change
of pants   just some 24-hour
coffee and a shot of

his tow-headed bastard daughter

his billfold all stained and coming
unstitched   poor guy

said he's clean   but all last night
he'd been heaving   right over there
behind those graves

So I brought him the raggedy quilt
I can't wash anymore

I let him pet my dog

I made up a name
for him to call me   Now I see him

looking a little bit worse   a little
bit worse

He's still so fucking
handsome   I make believe

I never met him

GOOD THINGS

All he has in the world
is a shopping cart, bed roll,
small spotted dog,
and her plastic dish.

When it's cold enough
that his glasses fog,
he covers her up
with his flak jacket,

tells her she has to
lie down, and she does,
and yawns; and watches
the world for him.

My Duck

The duck who followed me home
from the river was not
my duck. It marched along
past the open shops on its own
bright feet. I was just
its messiah. Thrusting its neck
to keep rhythm with each
exclaiming step, it belonged
to itself. I didn't toss flakes of scone
to it, or make those come-hither clicks
with my tongue's thick wing.
I only led it back
to the weary current and waded
straight in, that's all
I did; then I turned to make sure
that no one had questions.

N o w

I read to my dog from a take-out menu
so he can sleep. When he tires
of that, I talk to him
about nothing, and when I run out
of things to say, I make up words
to a song with whatever
array of notes and breath streams in

the way the clean wind did
as we rode once, and
I rolled down the window a hair
and he sat up without effort, glossy nose
in the speeding weather, eyes half closed
in the light that whizzed through his fur
like the hands of a friend

who had missed him.

RECEIVING THE HOST

When you could bear the sight of food no longer,
when the time had come, I brought the venison out
of the freezer, thawed it, broke it

like clouds of bread in the pot of autumn red water;
I cooked it and rinsed it of tallow, whistled it cool,
then fed it to you with my fingers, nugget by nugget,

waiting long enough between each one
you lolled over your tongue
with grateful reluctance, then swallowed;

and I blessed the doe who woke, and shook
the mist of tiny flies away from her head, and stood
in the light's good aim as if to watch you

close your eyes and eat.

HENRY

The vet tells me there won't be pain,
just a few last brain sparks; so
I hold my dog, give him his milkshake,
tickle the greasy depths of his ears;

then I say go ahead, could we please
do a back leg though; and the vet kneels down
as Henry's fur sheds onto the shirt
I knew I would wear for this;

and the pool-blue poison spreads first
over one startled web of his veins, then
through the skies of his blurring self;
and he struggles, for five wrong seconds,

free of my arms as if he could
saunter, panting, out where I will not
find him after I leave this blanket
on which a warm vacant body
will finally empty its bladder;

where I will not, cheek against its
checked heart, know him.

MILKSHAKE

He drank what I would want
if I were the dog laid out

on the hunter's blanket, worried
about one last thing:

that the faraway human
who twiddled my ears, and

blew the same three words
against my neck

and would not cry, might be afraid
I wasn't ready to hoist myself

with the old, old ease
from my body's rubble.

MABLE

Mable will need to lick her bed
and her fur and the pillow
she sleeps on, for all her life,
to calm herself, the long
avid oar of her tongue
rowing in circles, saying
the same word
over and over until I can read
the name I was meant to give her
so she can find her way dry
from the moss her paws taste of
without being called

POEM INSTEAD OF A NAP

I would live in your love as the sea-grasses live in
the sea,
Borne up by each wave as it passes, drawn down
by each wave that recedes . . . .

— *Sara Teasdale*

Mable lies down on my arm.
Beneath the idle tap of her heart, my hand
begins to fall asleep. I will not be able
to write, though my steno pad rests
on the window sill tingly with dust
beside me, my pen
on my pillow's lap. Not today, despite
the blank page, warm

as an animal's tawny chest. For my dog,
the hue of a beach on which only God
has set foot, is also falling asleep,
waking up, falling back
to sleep. In the kind-weather surf
of her breath, I too lift and drop:
a buoy with the sunlight's
dent of a smile.

BEATITUDE

You too might, in the holiest hour
of your life, allow a yearling bull
to nibble your hair and stroke
your ear with his hay-scented tongue.
If he does these things, draw him close,
let the tolerant wind of his nostrils
pray through your buttonholes.
Take off your mittens
and muss the crimps at the cliff
of his brow as the cold-weather
tear from his sagging eye
dries on its lash-blades; feed him
the crust from your bread, and receive
the blessing of him
as he swings his neck's beam
against your chest with no force,
no force at all.

THE NATIVITY OF THE ANIMALS

What other beasts slept,
or chewed, or flicked the gnats
from their cool ears, while far away
the Infant woke now and then
to the bitter dust of myrrh? Imagine

the goats the dawn of their slaying,
their piss-dank hooves tucked under
their bellies, twitching
with dreams they too might carry
a thin-clad girl who weighed

but a star's worth of light; and
the packs of matted coyotes
letting their prey retreat, unhurt;
or the young garter snake wrapped
like a lost sash tight to an apricot tree; or

the minnows' galaxies glinting up,
yet without souls.

III

The Stops

THE STOPS

I have to catch the 71 and the 55
city buses, both of them hourly,
to get to my father

there is no other way, though
I've lived in this city twenty years
and have many friends

so I bring a book
and something that no one
will notice me eating

I try to sit in one of the single seats
that doesn't have any graffiti
or damp spots, maybe

I get to read a page or two
or at least stay out of the way
of the boy whose pants are short,

who rides this route
every day, and shouts at himself
the names of all the stops

PANTS

I want a pair of rose-colored corduroy pants
like my father's that I can wear
day after day, the wale gone
smooth as a girl's cheek against
each knee, the waist loose, gnawed
in four places by rusting suspenders
that I can't work anymore
by myself, while I ache and wait
in my Lazyboy rocker, big-print book
sprawled flat, spine down in my lap as I close
the red, red eye of my face.

OLD WOMAN'S HEART

Once I could sit on my hair.
I collected combs and hand-painted
sticks from Russia to lift it aside
and let the moon out. Each night
I tucked a crinkled poppy
behind my ear to beckon a lover,
and lit the first cigarette of my life
off the earliest star. There's still a mark
on the small of my back
from the leaned-against sycamore.
Now I place on my bedside table this pebble
to which the river has done enough.
It is smooth as a shadow's thumb.
I push my gray bangs off my face
as if I'd a book to open in this
dim light, and somewhere to hide
from my only question: how
did I miss you?

ALTAR

Here is a pink ballerina barrette
for your lamb-white hair,

and here is a pretty new cross
for above your bed, and here

are three pills in a ruffled cup, and a bear
with chipped pearl eyes.

Here is a picture of you in your sundress
and sneakers, in Paris.

Here is a pillow
to prop you up, and a white

paper bracelet that won't slip off
your speckled wrist.

This is the prayer, but not the words.

DOROTHY

for Lee

First I opened her King James Bible
to a Psalm I didn't know
and read to her then I hummed
one old favorite of hers after another
the hymns the Broadway tunes
hoping at least to drown out
the game shows and intercoms just beyond
the great tent of her breathing
and after an hour or more
when her heart was done and dropped shut
and she lay deep and small
a blackening tear at her mouth's lid
I kept right on swabbing
the board of her tongue with sweet lemon Q-tips
and humming as best I could

Mother's Body, November

She can't read his lips or feel even one
of his words in the palm of her ear,

yet she must wish he would
stop shouting, because

no one is going to come for her
cleaned up body until

the dinner carts fill again
with plates of stone cold turnips,

and the same few bees tire out
in the bald lilacs.

CRYING

My father is crying because he has just been told
he can have his recliner from home.

He does not want his recliner from home, or
his desk, or his books, or pictures of us, or him,

when young. The things he loves that are there,
that he left, there, in that vacant place, behind,

must be angry at him. He misses them
but he can only stammer to please not bring them,

no. He is afraid of their shouting, and so he does not
want these things

in this room that has room now only for him, him
and his crying.

PAS DE DEUX

The attendant dips in to your room
and asks if we want ice cream.
You keep rocking your wheelchair
eight inches forward and eight
inches back. You swear at his
terrible English. Your voice

has soured, you tell me they've added
a pill. I have brought licorice
and library books. I open the bags
and line things up on your tray.
How hot you keep it here:

blinds clenched, fluorescent light
on the headstone of your face.
In its own stealthy time,
April will come. Even now

there are ants in the bathroom, streaming
from under the towel dispenser.
Yes, I will tell someone.
But for now we have this
to get good at:

you rock your wheelchair
eight inches forward and eight
again back; I sit with my jacket
unzipped on the end of your bed.

My father says

his mother's been and gone today.
She is so small, her coat

has dropped another stitch. She has
no shoes; she does not speak.

He points to where she was: exactly
there, no *there;* not listening

to him, but not not listening.
She tires easily,

he says, should not have come so far,
she needs to rest. He says

her knees were always sore. He tells
me this, I listen. And

he tells me this.

PUTTING AWAY MY BRAS

They are clean and papery gray and the lace, if
there is any lace, is torn, and the atrophied straps
are hitched tight in their plastic pincers.
The underwire on one
pokes up, no wonder the fire-
red itch on my rib. They are scentless
and warm from the dryer. Once they were pretty,
I bought them because I wished I were pretty.
Now the hooks grab and ravel
my socks. My bras are nothing at all

like my father's exact-fitting hand during beauty
pageants on TV. We sat on the couch
in his musty study and watched them;
he asked me why I couldn't
look like that, he dangled his arm over
my shoulder's ledge, he touched me and I
made believe he did not, I tried
his drink and chit-chatted with him
and my mother, and each of us picked the girl
we liked best, my tit staring into his palm.

SYMPHONY HALL

Every year it got more important
to take him out to the symphony, buy him
a seat from which he really believed
the concert mistress would see him; let him
not change his velcroed, scuffed shoes; maneuver him
over the slope of the floor in the balcony
into the right-lettered row; unbutton
his car coat and slide the sleeves down
his arms possessed by their tremors;
then ease him into the iron and velvet chair
and settle, beside him,
to leaf through the gorgeously printed notes
on each composer, the wars and the graceful goings
insane. But more than all this: the waning
house lights, the rustle of voices
dimmed, the last coughs and his own
gust of dark throat air.

Ushers

When it is late enough, they come
with their extinguished lamps
to draw the unresisting curtain
of your shirt. One has brought
a wastebasket and harvests
your discarded candy wrappers, then nods
to another — Barbadian, you guess —
his English listing like a yellow rowboat
against sea grass. And then
another: calm, austere,
one you haven't seen before
draws out the swabs and pin-lights
from their string pouch. Rest now,
let them lay your hands with reverence
beside your sore and white-streaked hips,
and work. Trust them.

DRINKING HOUR

He has trouble getting his fingers to curl
around the stem, for he has not had wine
in over a year, not any, and now
there's a table right here where his glass
can rest between sips of ordinary merlot,
and I have steadied him,
bone by bone, into the family's
oldest chair. And he blinks his lips
the way the skinny kitten, a feral, blinked
its eyes when I gave it the antibiotic and water
through a dropper, one tear a time.

BECAUSE I ASKED

If God were a small girl,
She would rest in my father's lap
for five or six minutes after
each sponge bath;

and tuck the Buffalo nickel
back behind his warm ear
so he'll know where it is.

REQUEST

Lord, at the end of the world,
let me spread out my coat

and sit down on the floor
in the back

of a secondhand bookstore,

and lower my head and rejoice
in the glory

of all my unreadiness, then

take off my old, unfixable glasses.

WALKING AN OLD WOMAN INTO THE SEA

She doesn't need her bathing cap
but she wants it on, the rubber peony
over one temple, the ear flaps up;

and the scratched yellow goggles
that won't get wet today
belong right here around her neck.

She can't hear the gulls' beady voices
yack over our sandwich crusts,

or the sea, out late again, tripping home
over its skirts;

and she frets about where I have left
her terrycloth jacket and watch.

But she knows by the popping
of stones and shell bits
under her flip-flops, and by my own

aged hands that grip the slack
elastic waist of her suit,

that this is a swim-day, no matter
how long the water
will have to wait.

TALKING TO MY FATHER ABOUT GOD

My father cannot spell *world*. He tries,
but can't find the *d*, so we have our lunch.
I fish a pin-striped bug from my warm
ginger ale, something at least
a finger can do to help. I pass it to him
as it flicks the fizz off its legs. He's folded
his walker against the empty chair
between us. The dining hall's thick
with the waltzing of trays and their waitresses.
He has perfect vision but can't see
the stripes, or the nib of the bug's fine bottom
that might be a stinger. So I decide on my own
it's a she, and that makes him somehow glad.
Then I watch the single quotes of her wings
lift off around what's left for us:
world, most of it.

ABOUT THE AUTHOR

Frannie Lindsay's first book of poems, *Where She Always Was*, was selected by J. D. McClatchy as the 2004 recipient of the May Swenson Award sponsored by Utah State University Press. She has been awarded fellowships from the Massachusetts Cultural Council and the National Endowment for the Arts.

Lindsay holds an MFA from the Iowa Writers' Workshop, has been awarded residencies at the MacDowell and Millay Colonies, and at Yaddo, and is also a classical pianist. She lives in Cambridge, Massachusetts, with her retired greyhounds.

This book was typeset in Centaur, a Venetian oldstyle typeface designed by Bruce Rogers in 1914 for a translation of De Guerin's *Le Centaure*. The font is based on the type designs of fifteenth-century printer Nicolas Jensen. The typeface's companion italics are based on Arrighi, drawn by Frederic Warde in 1925 and based on the letterforms of sixteenth-century calligrapher Ludovico degli Arrighi.